The Church that Jesus is Building

Doug Roberts

The Church that Jesus is Building

by Doug Roberts

Published by:
> *Doug Roberts Publishing*
> *P.O. Box 321*
> *Frederick, Oklahoma 73542*

Unless otherwise indicated, scripture quotations are taken from the New American Standard Bible® (NASB), Copyright © 1960, 1962, 1963, 1968, 1971, 1972, 1973, 1975, 1977, 1995 by The Lockman Foundation. Used by permission. www.Lockman.org

Printed in the United States of America

ISBN: 978-0-9825992-5-9

I thank Ed Chinn, Tim and Laurie Thornton, Shellie Kushnerick, Fred White, and Rob Hatch for all the work they did in helping me transfer the things in my heart to print.

I want to say thank you to the most amazing woman, my wife Rita. Without her my journey would have not been complete.

Table of Contents

Chapter 1: What, Where, and Who is the Church?

Have you ever wondered what the church is? Over my years of ministry, I've learned that many people think they know more than they do, and much of what they know is not true. For example, many know that the church is a *building*, and they know what Christians do on Sunday mornings and Wednesday nights in those buildings. Is that really what we learn about the church from the scriptures? What do the scriptures teach about the church and about what God is calling her to be?

First, the church is a body, not a building. Defining the church as a building is the first assumption, illusion, and false priority we need to let go of in order to better agree with the Father's heart for his people. Matthew 16:18 contains the first use of the word church in the New Testament, the Greek word, *ekklesia*, which means "the called-out ones." Jesus said He will build His church—the assembly of the called-out ones—and the gates of hell will not overpower it.

The Church in Time and Space

The Bible speaks of Jesus as being seated in heavenly places (Ephesians 1:20). It also says that we have been raised up and seated "with Him in the heavenly places" (Ephesians 2:6). Heavenly places refer to the realm of eternity, the dimension where all things are completed in Him. From that eternal place, we all dwell on the earth, in time and space. In other words, we walk out our eternal *position* within our earthly *conditions.* Jesus, the head of the church, sees His church—His people, His called-out ones—as she is in her perfect and completed state in eternity. However, He also sees her coming to perfection here in time and space.

> We walk out our eternal position within our earthly conditions. So, Jesus, the head of the church, sees His church as she is in her perfect and completed state in eternity. However, He also sees her coming to perfection in time and space.

That "space" has four realms:

1.   The Whole Earth

As we told you, the first mention of church in the New Testament (Matthew 16:18) refers to the church in the whole earth—the "church universal." When Jesus looks down from heaven, what does

He see? He sees His church. He doesn't just see all these different forms of what the world calls the church. He sees His one church.

2. A Region

Acts 9:31 contains the second reference to church in the scriptures: "So the church throughout all Judea and Galilee and Samaria enjoyed peace." This passage refers to the church in a region or the church in a larger area. So, we start with the church in the whole earth, and then we see that the church can be seen in a region of the whole earth.

3. A City

The third time scripture mentions the church is in Acts 13:1, referring to the church in a particular city (Antioch). So again we start with the church in the whole earth and in that church are churches in the region. In the church in the region, there are churches in a city.

4. A House

Romans 16:3-5, Colossians 4:15, and Philippians 2 all talk about churches that meet in houses. So even here, in the midst of the city, you have a form of the church meeting in homes.

The church in time and space is found in four different forms or geographic realms, but they are all expressions of the church in the

3

whole earth—the called-out ones. And, of course, there is one church, one body, and one head, but there are many members in the different forms of the church. Jesus died for the whole earth. Anyone who believes in his or her heart and confesses with his or her mouth that Jesus is Lord is part of His church.

Who is the Church?

When the Bible speaks of the church in any of those four realms, it is always referring to a group of believers, never a building. It's never referring to denominations. The church is people. We are the church. When you accept Jesus Christ as your Lord and Savior, you become part of His church—the church that He is building—and the gates of hell cannot overpower it.

> When you accept Jesus Christ as your Lord and Savior, you become part of His church—the church that He is building.

When I was growing up we sang a little song.

Here is the church.

Here is the steeple.

Open the door.

Here's all the people.

Remember that one? When most of us think of church, we picture a steeple on top of a building because that is the tradition we have been taught. When God speaks of the church, He speaks of the people. Jesus didn't die for brick and mortar. He is not coming back for brick and mortar. *We* are the living stones that He is building together for His own holy habitat. When the Bible talks about the church, it's referring to the people, the body of Christ properly related to the head, which is Jesus.

Chapter 2: What is the Body of Christ?

When my ear itches, my head tells my finger that my ear itches and to scratch it. My finger obeys; it goes right to my ear and scratches it. Does your body do that? When your ear itches does your head tell your finger to scratch it? Does your finger obey? See, the natural body has no problem relating to the head. My body understands that my head rules the rest of my body.

Wouldn't it be beautiful if the spiritual body acted the same way? When the head—Jesus—tells the "finger" to scratch the "ear," what happens? Too often the finger says, "Now, wait a minute. You know that ear has been listening to some things it doesn't need to hear. It's been listening to some things I don't agree with. I cannot, in good conscience, obey what the head is telling me to do. In fact, I think it must be the devil telling me to scratch that ear because Jesus wouldn't tell me to to anything I don't agree with."

When your head tells one of your fingers to scratch the ear, does your toe jump up to do the job because it wants to be the finger? Is your toe in rebellion? Does your toe get jealous and begin striving with the finger? No, of course not. That would be a dysfunctional body, wouldn't it? So why does the Lord's body so often act like that?

Christ is the head of the body, and His body must understand that it is under His rulership.

That Which Every Part Supplies

Christ is the head of His body, the church, but we know from 1 Corinthians 12:12-13 that the body has many members: "For even as the body is one and yet has many members, and all the members of the body, though they are many, are one body, so also is Christ. For by one Spirit we were all baptized into one body, whether Jews or Greeks." Whether Baptist or Methodist, Pentecostal or Catholic, tongue talkers or no-tongue talkers, "we were all baptized into one body . . . whether slaves or free"—whether blue or green—"we were all made to drink of one Spirit." Isn't that what it says? It says we were all baptized into the one body.

For the body is not one member, but many. We can clearly see that the body is designed so that we need one another. God didn't make the natural body to be independent of itself, did He? If you lose your arm, can your body still function? Yes, but in a weakened state. If my right arm was not there, the rest of my body would adjust, but there would be some things I couldn't do. Of course, that arm would be sorely missed.

But in the spiritual body, we sometimes just cut off the arm because we don't like it; we don't appreciate the value it brings and we can't imagine that we would ever need it or miss it. Isn't that an amazing contrast? Remember, the Word says, "For even as the body is one and yet has many members, and all the members of the body, though they are many, are all one body, so also is Christ."

What is the church? The people. Who is the head? Jesus. How many members are there? Many. Does every member have the same function? No. Each part of the spiritual body is needed by every other part in the same way that each part of the physical body is needed by every other part. We need each other. As Ephesians 4:16 says, in my own paraphrase, that which every joint supplies brings the fullness of the Father. I can't bring the full manifold wisdom of God; I can just bring my portion.

Colossians 3:24 says that there is an inheritance stored up in the saints. Maybe I am a selfish man, but I want all that God has for me. That's why I love relationships in the Lord's body. I love them because in my relationships I get to tap into the inheritance that is stored up in you; I get to tap into the gift that you are to me. You can see why the devil doesn't

I love relationships in the Lord's body. I love them because in my relationships I get to tap into the inheritance that is stored up in you; I get to tap into the gift that you are to me.

want the body to fellowship with one another. When we begin to fellowship with one another and every joint begins to supply its portion, then the body is healthy.

When I go to a doctor because my chest hurts, the doctor checks me over and then says, "Drop your drawers."

I say, "Doc, my bottom is not hurting. It is my chest that is hurting." But I drop my drawers and he sticks a needle in my *derriere*. And now I leave with my *derriere* hurting, too. But all of a sudden the medicine he gave me begins to go through my body to the infected area and that infected area starts to feeling better. The *derriere* had to suffer a little bit to bring healing to what needed healing.

But what happens in the spiritual body?

Is the Church a Dysfunctional Body?

Too often when one part hurts, the other parts rejoice. They judge the hurt part and say, "Praise God, we are not like that part of the body. Lord, we knew we were right and they were wrong. Judge them some more."

Those parts are not willing to be the "derriere" that gets the shot. They rejoice when others suffer.

Can you see that when we act like that we don't understand the body of Christ? We are joined one to another. We are not independent of one another. When you are independent—when you are cut off from the rest of the body—does any life actually get to you? No! It cannot because there is no joint and no connection.

What happens to a part of the natural body that is cut off? It dies. It stinketh. It is not good for anything. And there is a lot of the spiritual body that stinks because it is not connected to the rest of its body. It is not joined one to another. How can the Father bless that which is isolated?

Some people pray for revival, asking the Father to do something, and then when He starts doing it down the street at another part of the body, they get upset. They say, "Well, Father? Why aren't you doing that great thing here? Those people don't even believe in the fullness of what you are doing in the earth today. Why are you blessing them and doing wonderful things in their midst?"

Maybe He's blessing those other groups simply because someone asked Jesus to do something in His body. The truth is, often we want Jesus do something in our *building*. But when He starts building His church, we get mad because it is

I've never known a time when one part of my body desired to hurt another part of my body.

not in our facility.

I've never known a time when one part of my body desired to hurt another part of my body. When I have accidentally hit my finger with a hammer during a building project, my hand immediately drops that hammer and holds the finger so tightly. My hand seems to say, "Oh! I am sorry. I didn't mean to do that. I am hurting with you."

Sometimes in the spiritual body, however, when that hammer hits that finger, the other parts of the body often say, "Praise God! Thank you for judging the finger, Lord. Hit them again." I promise you that if I actually hit your finger with a hammer, you are not going to tell me to hit you again. It is amazing that the natural body responds to one another in ways that the spiritual body does not. Ephesians 4:15-16 says, "We are to grow up in all aspects into Him who is the head, even Christ, from whom the whole body, being fitted and held together by what every joint supplies, according to the proper working of each individual part, causes the growth of the body for the building up of itself in love."

We are to grow up in all aspects into Him, Jesus, the head, not a denomination. We are not to grow up into our interpretations of scripture. We are not to grow up into our understanding of what we think we might know. We are to grow up into Jesus. When you grow up into Jesus, then you are going to have relationships with one with another because we are all members of His body.

When I was saved, I was a lover of people. I loved everybody. If they knew Jesus, I loved them. All of a sudden, people started to warn me: "Well, you need to watch those people over there because they believe that people can have a demon." Or some would say, "You need to watch those people over there because they believe you can speak in tongues." Others would tell me, "You need to watch those people over there because they believe that God can still heal today." So instead of remaining a lover, I became a watcher. Then I started limiting my fellowship to people that agreed with me. I would test them in my mind: Do you agree with me in this? Yeah? Okay, then I can fellowship with you. Do you agree with me in that? No? Then we cannot be brother and sister.

The truth is, it's stupid for me to think that I have all of the truth. This is my 43rd year in the ministry and I am still learning the ways of the Lord. Just when I think I know something, the Holy Spirit gives me more understanding and I realize that I didn't even know what I thought I knew. (However, there are two things I know for sure: The Father loves me and the Father is killing me, because He wants me to be like Jesus. He has been faithful in both of those areas.) Let me reiterate this: We should be connected enough that when one part suffers, all suffer. When one part rejoices, all rejoice.

Who is the Head of the Church?

Ephesians 1:22-23 says, "And He put all things in subjection under His feet, and gave Him as head over all things to the church, which is His body, the fullness of Him who fills all in all."

Now, I know the Father has been around a long time. He is called "the Ancient of Days" in Daniel. But I don't think He is senile. Do you? I think He knows what He is doing. And He has written here, by the Holy Spirit, that He has put all things in subjection under His feet. And

He gave Him, Jesus, as head over all things to the church, which is His body and the fullness of Him who fills all in all.

> Who is the head? Jesus.
>
> Who is the body? We are.
>
> How many heads are there? One.
>
> How many bodies are there? One.

Colossians 1:18 says, "He is the head of the body, the church." Jesus is the head of His body.

14

Chapter 3: What is the House of God?

So then you are no longer strangers and aliens, but you are fellow citizens with the saints, and are of God's household, having been built on the foundation of the apostles and prophets, Christ Jesus Himself being the corner stone, in whom the whole building, being fitted together, is growing into a holy temple in the Lord, in whom you are being built together into a dwelling place of God in the Spirit.
—Ephesians 2:19-22

Where does God dwell? In the church! Where is the church? You are looking at it, baby!

You are Part of His House

Do we understand that life —His life—dwells within us? Jesus lives within you. You are the expression of God on the earth. The facility you worship in—that Gothic temple or that steel structure in a strip mall—isn't the expression of Jesus on the earth. You are.

The world drives by and they see all the buildings that announce, "First Holy Church" or "Second Holy Church" or "Full Gospel Fire and Brimstone Church." And the world wonders why we're so divided.

15

Living Stones

I Peter 2:5 says, "You also, as living stones, are being built up as a spiritual house for a holy priesthood, to offer up sacrifices acceptable to God through Christ Jesus." Each stone is an important part to the whole structure. What happens if a stone is missing? That leaves a hole in the wall. Think about it this way: If you look at a brick wall, you can see that, with most bricklaying patterns, each brick has a personal relationship with six other bricks. If you remove a brick, then you weaken all the bricks around it.

Let's also see and rejoice that, in many masonry styles, the building stones come in every shape and size and color. The living stones—the people of God—are also very different from one another. They have different gifts and personalities and even represent different heritages and destinies.

A man told me one time that if two people were exactly alike then one of them was not needed. It would be a scary place if everyone was like me or you. So why do we try to bring everyone to be like us instead of bringing them into being complete in Christ? Just like every part of the physical body has a function to perform, every part of the spiritual body also has a unique function. Each member has a role, a duty, that is vital to the life of the body of Christ, the church. Each member must contribute his or her part. Each member is needed. Each member is necessary and unique. We need each one to supply his or her part to the body of Christ.

Chapter 4: How and Where Do You Fit?

Since we have gifts that differ according to the grace given to us, each of us is to exercise them accordingly: if prophecy, according to the proportion of his faith; if service, in his serving; or he who teaches, in his teaching; or he who exhorts, in his exhortation; he who gives, with liberality; he who leads, with diligence; he who show mercy, with cheerfulness. — Romans 12:6-8

What is your part? What is the grace that God has given you? What has God predestined you to be in Christ before the foundation of the world? What has he called you to be?

Are You a Trustee of the Toilet?

What if His grace on you and His design for you was that you should produce the best and cleanest toilets in town? If you are walking in that design, your clean toilet can be part of the salvation experience for the lost when they go into the bathroom because you did your job as unto the Lord and with all your might and with all your strength! The toilet that you clean is going to be the "righteous-est" toilet in the county. When people go in there, they'll come face-to-face with a loving God because you prayed over that toilet, "Lord, I pray that everyone that comes into this bathroom will be confronted by your love and your goodness and your mercy. Lord, everyone that washes their hands in this sink, let them be cleansed with the blood of your Son and the love that you have."

Anoint that bathroom with prayer because that bathroom is your portion.

Of course, many would say that they want to have a more prominent ministry than trustee of the toilet. That's fine if He gave you the grace to do something else. Trust me, though, you don't want to be in a place that you don't have grace for. You can only do what God has given you grace to do. You can only fill up the place where God has placed you. The Word says that God places the members of the

> You can only do what God has given you grace to do. You can only fill up a place where God has placed you.

body where HE sees fit. You and I don't even have a right to be what we want to be. We must be what He sees and chooses us to be.

I Corinthians 12:4-11 says, "There are varieties of gifts, but the same Spirit. And there are varieties of ministries, and the same Lord. There are varieties of effects, but the same God who works all things in all persons. But to each one is given the manifestation of the Spirit for the common good. For to one is given the word of wisdom through the Spirit, and to another the word of knowledge according to the same Spirit; to another faith by the same Spirit, to another gifts of

19

healing by the one Spirit, and to another the effecting of miracles, and to another prophecy, to another the distinguishing of spirits, to another various kinds of tongues, and to another the interpretation of tongues. But one and the same Spirit works all these things, distributing to each one individually just as He wills."

Ephesians 4:1-3 says, "Therefore, I, the prisoner for the Lord, implore you to walk in a manner worthy of the calling with which you have been called, with all humility and gentleness, with patience, showing tolerance for one another in love, being diligent to preserve the unity of the Spirit in the bond of peace."

What is the Measure of your Success?

How many parts of the body are there? Many

How many bodies are there? One

How many heads does the body have? One

The natural body can understand that. If we could transfer the simplicity of the natural body into the spiritual body, we would quit devouring one another. Jealousy would stop. We would quit envying and striving with one another. We would get our minds off the temporal things as the measure of our success. We would get our minds onto the eternal purpose that God has created us for, which is to bring glory and honor unto Him, and to establish and make disciples that growth might come. *That* is succeeding in the Lord!

If the world sees the church loving one another, they will know that God sent His Son (John 17:21).

When the body becomes the body and the church becomes the church and it begins to walk in relationship and accountability and begins seeing the head (Christ) glorified, the world will know that God sent His Son. They will see us loving one another and working together, not as a dysfunctional body, but as one body with one purpose: to fulfill the will and purpose of our head.

Are we going to get there? I believe we are. Is it going to be in my generation? I don't know. Am I going to be able to see it? I don't know. I am praying that I will see it. I know it is the heart of God, but what is it going to take? It is going to take us dying to ourselves and abiding in Him, abiding in the branch. If we understand John 15, we will know that, unless we abide in Him, we can't be the expression of Him in the earth.

Be Who He Called You to Be

So church, be the church. If you have heard anything from me, be joined to one another. Invest in a vision larger than yourself. Have the heart of the Father for your area and begin to work together.

> Is everyone going to meet in the same building? No.
>
> Is everybody going to have the same doctrine? No.
>
> Is everybody going to be in agreement? No.
>
> Can everybody walk in fellowship in the Lord Jesus Christ? Yes!

If we only know Jesus Christ and Him crucified, we can fellowship right there together. If that is where we have our point of relationship, then we can walk together in Him. Am I going to put you down because you don't do what I do? No! You can't walk in things until God gives you the grace to do them.

You can't be someone other than yourself. You cannot do what someone else is called to do. You can only be who He called you to be.

There is only one way to the Father, and that is through Jesus. There is only one way for forgiveness of sin, and that is with the shedding of His blood. If that is all we can fellowship in, that is enough because that is eternal. Let's see how we can begin to be joined to one another instead of being divided from one another. Let's begin to see what the heart of Father is for us, our local expressions of the church, and our cities.

I pray that the amazing grace of the master, Jesus Christ, the extravagant love of God the Father, the intimate friendship of the Holy Spirit, be with all of you.

Group Discussion Guide

My hope and purpose for this book is to see it become seed in the rich soil of human hearts. These questions were put together by some brothers and sisters to help you work these truths into your life.

1. Why do you think physical things that we associate with church—buildings, pews, classrooms, choir lofts—have such a hold on our minds?

2. Can you explain the difference between the church in the realm of eternity and the church on earth?

3. What are the four geographic realms of the church here on earth?

4. How does a person become part of the Lord's church?

5. The scriptures use the human body to explore how the members of the Lord's body relate to each other. How have you seen the similarities/differences played out in your own life? Can you talk about it?

6. Can we belong to a denomination and still be part of His *one* church? Explain.

7. Using Ephesians 4:15-16, explain how the life of Jesus reaches all the members of His church?

8. What kinds of things and practices might contribute to the world seeing the church as dysfunctional and dangerous?

9. Have you experienced a similar shift from a being a lover of God's people into being a suspicious watcher of others? Why?

What contributed to it? Take some time now to repent and return to loving the whole church.

10. How can we best see and honor the Lord as the head of His church?

11. According to Ephesians 2:19-22, we are all part of God's "dwelling place." What does that look like in your own church? In your own personal life?

12. What does it mean to be a "living stone"? Are you and your local church connected to other "stones" in a way that strengthens the whole building? Have you or your local church separated yourselves from others in a way that weakens the whole building?

13. What does it mean to operate within the measure, or portion, of our grace? Take some time to ask the Lord to reveal your portion to you. How can you adjust your life to apply yourself to that portion?

14. Do you think we make the church too complicated? If so, why? If not, why not?

15. Using John 17:21, talk about the greatest evidence that we are joined to Chris

www.ingramcontent.com/pod-product-compliance
Lightning Source LLC
Chambersburg PA
CBHW020448030426
42337CB00014B/1449